T0059301

What Is
the Declaration
of Independence?

by Michael C. Harris

illustrated by Jerry Hoare

Penguin Workshop

Dedicated to Nathan Branch, a freed slave
who in 1868 built the home I currently live in,
in Evanston, Illinois. It took most of his life
to realize the aspiration that the Declaration of
Independence promised in 1776—MCH

PENGUIN WORKSHOP
An Imprint of Penguin Random House LLC, New York

If you purchased this book without a cover, you should be aware that this book is stolen property. It was reported as "unsold and destroyed" to the publisher, and neither the author nor the publisher has received any payment for this "stripped book."

Penguin supports copyright. Copyright fuels creativity, encourages diverse voices, promotes free speech, and creates a vibrant culture. Thank you for buying an authorized edition of this book and for complying with copyright laws by not reproducing, scanning, or distributing any part of it in any form without permission. You are supporting writers and allowing Penguin to continue to publish books for every reader.

The publisher does not have any control over and does not assume any responsibility for author or third-party websites or their content.

Text copyright © 2016 by Michael C. Harris.
Illustrations copyright © 2016 by Penguin Random House LLC. All rights reserved.
Published by Penguin Workshop, an imprint of Penguin Random House LLC, New York.
PENGUIN and PENGUIN WORKSHOP are trademarks of Penguin Books Ltd.
WHO HQ & Design is a registered trademark of Penguin Random House LLC.
Printed in the USA.

Visit us online at www.penguinrandomhouse.com.

Library of Congress Control Number: 2016011713

ISBN 9780448486925 (paperback)   20 19 18 17 16 15 14 13
ISBN 9780399542305 (library binding)   10 9 8 7 6 5 4 3

Contents

What Is the Declaration of Independence?

June 26, 1776, Philadelphia

The June heat in Philadelphia was blistering. Even before the sun came up, it was hot. Thomas Jefferson of Virginia did his best to stay cool as he wrote in the room he had rented on Market Street. He was writing a letter. But it was no ordinary letter.

Along with Jefferson, important men from all thirteen American colonies had come to Philadelphia. They planned to do something brave and dangerous. The colonies were declaring their freedom from Great Britain. They were going to create a new country—the United States of America.

Thomas Jefferson was chosen to write a public letter to the British king listing all the reasons why people in America were rebelling. Jefferson also wanted the letter to show other countries in Europe why this was the right decision for America. It took Jefferson—with help from others—only a couple of weeks to finish one of the most important documents in history: the Declaration of Independence.

Sending an announcement like this—a declaration—meant that the colonists in America would go to war. The British army was large and powerful. The colonists didn't even have an army. The chances were slim that the Americans could win. Many would certainly die. And even if by some chance the colonists did win their freedom, could thirteen different colonies create a new country together?

For two weeks Jefferson worked on the Declaration of Independence. He sat at the small desk that he had made by hand. He wrote in ink on large sheets of paper with his quill pen.

Each day Jefferson would discuss the ideas for the declaration with some of the other men who had gathered in Philadelphia. After these

talks, Jefferson would sometimes tear up his most recent draft of the declaration and start over.

He wanted to get every word just right. The declaration had to explain more than why the colonies could no longer live under British rule. More importantly, it had to tell the world what this new country hoped to stand for. It would not have a king. It would set up a government in which ordinary men decided the laws.

After the Declaration of Independence was finished, it was signed on July 4, 1776. It has become one of the most important statements of freedom. It has inspired people around the globe to fight for their freedom as well. Thomas Jefferson wrote, "We hold these truths to be self-evident, that all men are created equal." This meant that this new United States would treat everyone the same. Jefferson may not have realized how powerful those simple words would be for hundreds of years to come.

Were All Men Equal?

Jefferson's famous phrase about all men being "created equal" didn't hold true in the American colonies. In 1776 there were about half a million African slaves belonging to white colonists. Jefferson himself owned slaves. So did many of the other men who signed the Declaration of Independence. In his first version of the declaration, Jefferson included antislavery language. But too many of the signers didn't want to end slavery. So there is no mention of it. Jefferson did free a few of his slaves. So did many of the other men who signed the Declaration of Independence.

CHAPTER 1
A Battle for America

After Columbus set foot in the "New World" in 1492, many European countries wanted to rule different parts of North America. Great Britain, France, and Spain controlled almost the entire continent.

Great Britain had thirteen colonies along the east coast, where most settlers lived. France—Great Britain's great rival—had the largest area of land, north and west of the colonies. But not many settlers lived there. Same with Spain—it had a bigger chunk of land than Great Britain but with far fewer people.

This map shows what land belonged to France, Great Britain, and Spain. The striped areas were regions that different countries claimed to own.

In 1754, Great Britain tried to grab more of North America by invading lands controlled by the French. This led to a war known as the French and Indian War.

A young lieutenant colonel named George Washington served in the British army, fighting against the French.

Most American colonists wanted Great Britain to win the war with France. And, after many years, it did. Great Britain doubled the area of land it controlled.

Before the French and Indian War . . . and after

During the war, many British soldiers were sent to America to fight. That had been very costly. King George III had to borrow massive amounts of money from other countries.

After winning the war, King George III had to pay back what he owed. In the king's mind, he had been defending the American colonies against the French. So he expected the colonies to help with the war debt. This angered people in America.

It wasn't the colonists' idea to start the war. It had been fought because the king wanted more land. So why should Americans have to pay?

George Washington, British Soldier

The son of a successful Virginia farmer, George Washington was only twenty-two years old when he led 150 British soldiers against French troops along the Ohio River. This was at the very beginning of the French and Indian War. His troops were defeated by the French army, and Washington had to surrender. He was ashamed. A year later, Washington returned to the same area to fight, and once again the French overpowered his forces. Washington had two horses shot from underneath him. The best he could do was lead the defeated British soldiers back to safety.

Although praised for his bravery in the war, Washington retired from the British army in 1758. He returned to his farm in Virginia. However, seventeen years later, Washington became commander in chief of the Continental Army. Now he was fighting *against* Great Britain.

King George III didn't listen to that argument. The British government—called Parliament—taxed the American colonists heavily to pay for the war debts. The American colonists had no one representing them in Parliament. It met in London, more than three thousand miles away and across the Atlantic Ocean. The colonists had no way to argue against the high taxes.

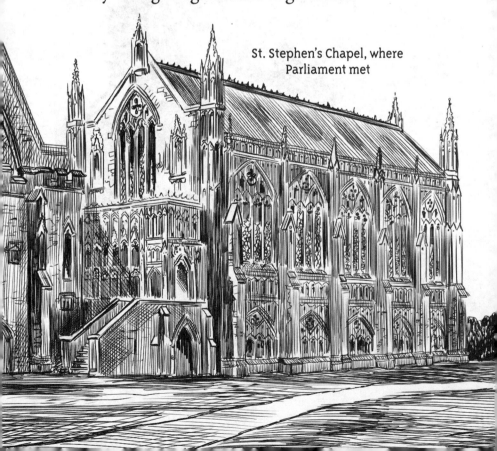

St. Stephen's Chapel, where Parliament met

House of Burgesses

Did Parliament decide on all laws governing the colonies? No. There were local governments with men elected by their fellow colonists.

In Virginia, for example, there was the House of Burgesses. However, none of these groups had much power. In each colony, a royal governor made all the important decisions. Whatever the governor decided should be the law *was* the law. And he was appointed by the king. So Great Britain always had the final say about all laws and taxes. This got people in the colonies angry. Very angry.

CHAPTER 2
Taxes and More Taxes

Besides taxing colonists, King George did other things that made the situation in America grow even more tense. In 1761 he ordered a renewal of the Writs of Assistance, which were a kind of search warrant. British customs officers and soldiers were allowed to search shops, warehouses, and even people's homes. This was to make sure colonists were only buying things

made in Great Britain or by the British. If goods from other countries were found, the shopkeeper or homeowner had to pay a fine to the king.

The colonists were furious. It was one thing to search a warehouse or even a shop, but searching people's homes was an outrage! James Otis, a lawyer from Massachusetts, went to court. He tried to get the searches stopped. He is often credited with one of the most important lines in American history: "Taxation without representation is tyranny." This idea—that it's completely wrong to tax people without letting them have a voice in the matter—would become a rallying cry for the American colonists.

James Otis

But King George III didn't seem to care what the colonists thought. He needed more and more money, so Great Britain's Parliament passed more and more taxes on the colonies.

The Sugar Act of 1764 hit the colonists hard. It was a tax on all sugar, molasses, wine, rum, and even some lumber and iron. Every home in the colonies used sugar every single day.

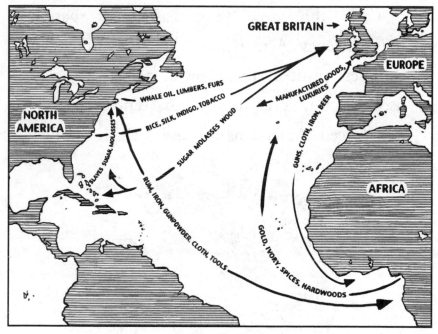

Flow of Goods

The sugar tax hurt the economy of the colonies. Rum was big business in the colonies, as it was used to trade for African slaves. Lumber and iron were important businesses, too—and they were heavily taxed now. But Great Britain couldn't care less—it wanted as much money as it could get out of colonists.

Later the same year, Parliament passed the Currency Act. Before this, the American colonies printed their own money. It was used to buy everyday goods. The Currency Act forced Americans to use British money.

British coin, circa 1760s

This angered the colonists because their colonial money was now worthless. People in the colonies took to the streets to protest against the king and Parliament. But this was only the beginning—can you believe it gets worse?

The Stamp Act of 1765 was like an explosion in the American colonies.

British stamp

Up until the Stamp Act, Americans mostly paid taxes to Great Britain on items sold to other countries. For example, if a merchant in Pennsylvania sold lumber to a Spanish company, the Pennsylvania company had to pay Great Britain a tax on that sale. But any lumber that the Pennsylvania merchant sold to other colonial customers was not taxed.

But with the Stamp Act, colonists paid a tax on items sold in America. For instance, anything printed on paper—newspapers, contracts, wills, even playing cards—had to have a British stamp. And there was a price for the stamp. If a newspaper cost one pence before the Stamp Act, afterward it cost two pence. The Stamp Act affected *every* colonist. And all of them hated it.

Riots broke out across the colonies. In Boston, a man named Samuel Adams urged colonists to fight back. First they stormed the office of the

Samuel Adams

New Yorkers ransack the home of Major Thomas James

British tax commissioner. (The commissioner collected all the taxes for Great Britain.) Then protesters went to his home. He was so frightened by the crowd that he quit his job the very next day. In New York, two thousand angry colonists ransacked the house of British major Thomas James. Why? He boasted that he would ram the Stamp Tax down colonists' throats at the point of a sword.

It was only after colonists stopped buying British goods that Parliament ended the Stamp Act. The plan had backfired.

Did that put an end to the trouble? No!

King George and Parliament came up with a new tax scheme. It was called the Townshend Acts. These 1767 acts taxed all colonial paint, oil, and glass. And one other thing: tea.

Again people in the colonies rebelled. They protested in the streets and they boycotted—meaning they refused to buy—British goods.

This was hard on many households. Only the British sold certain things that most colonial families depended on. It was not easy to give these things up. What colonists minded the most was doing without tea.

Tea was a favorite drink in the colonies. Even though it was expensive, most colonists were regular tea drinkers. Boiling water was a common way to purify water. So in every cup of tea, colonists were drinking both clean water and a delicious-tasting beverage.

Most tea came to America on British ships that had first picked it up in other parts of the world. Now colonists found ways to get tea illegally. Some tea was shipped in from other countries without the British authorities ever finding out. Some tea was grown in America, including teas made of mint or chicory.

The colonists agreed to tough it out and continue the boycott. It was important to make the king and Parliament understand how fed up they were over these taxes.

Eventually, the boycott was a success. Or mostly a success. Once again Great Britain was losing too much money. So Parliament did away with the taxes on glass, paper, and sugar in 1770. In fact, they got rid of almost everything in the Townshend Acts. Only one tax was left in place: the tax on tea. Surely the colonists would see how reasonable the king and the British government were being.

Tea in the Colonies

The tradition of drinking tea came across the Atlantic Ocean with the first British settlers of the "New World." Tea became popular throughout the colonies. Big cities like New York and Philadelphia had many tea gardens where tea was served in the finest porcelain, or sometimes in silver cups. Even in tiny rural towns, American colonists enjoyed drinking tea. If you drank tea, whether in a fancy tea garden or at your kitchen table, it was a sign that you were doing well and were rather sophisticated.

CHAPTER 3
Blood in Boston

Boston, Massachusetts, in early 1770 was a tense city. *Very* tense. There were so many protests and gatherings that Great Britain sent hundreds of soldiers to the city to keep the peace. Instead, seeing so many soldiers in their streets only made Bostonians even angrier.

In late February, a crowd gathered at the home of a British tax collector. Rather than trying to calm down the colonists, an officer came out and fired his gun at the crowd. An eleven-year-old boy named Christopher Seider was killed.

All of Boston was shocked. Even the royal governor of Massachusetts, a man chosen by the king, was outraged. A record number of

Bostonians attended the boy's funeral. The sad event was as much a political protest as a time to mourn the death of a child.

Only a week after Christopher Seider's funeral, a Boston merchant insulted a British soldier. The soldier struck the man with his rifle.

In a flash, two hundred Bostonians were at the scene. Then a few more British soldiers arrived. Suddenly the crowd began to throw sticks, stones, and snowballs at them. When one of the soldiers was hit, the others pointed their guns and began firing.

Three colonists died on the spot. One was Crispus Attucks, a sailor of African and Native American descent. Of the eight wounded, two died within days. That brought the total number of colonists killed to five.

The tragic incident quickly became known as the Boston Massacre. And it fueled the colonists' hatred of the British.

News of the massacre spread quickly. There were more angry protests against the British in cities across the colonies. In Boston, the royal governor promised a full investigation of the murders. Even he knew that the British soldiers had gone too far.

Eight British soldiers were brought to trial for the murders. It is safe to bet they were among the most hated men in Boston. Probably many colonists hoped they would hang for their crime. But the soldiers' lawyer was determined to see that they received a fair trial.

Who was their lawyer?

John Adams.

John Adams

This may seem surprising, since John Adams was very much against British rule. And, indeed, many Bostonians were angry with Adams for defending the British soldiers. But Adams felt that everyone deserved to be fairly represented in court. So he took the job, even after getting death threats. In the end, the jury decided that six of the eight soldiers were not guilty. Only two soldiers were convicted of murder and executed.

The trial made Adams an unpopular man in Boston. He lost a lot of clients, and his family suffered. But right up until the day he died, Adams believed he had done the right thing.

CHAPTER 4
The Boston Tea Party

Sam Adams wasn't going to let a trial put the Boston Massacre to rest. He egged on his fellow citizens, reminding them all to "remember the

bloody massacre!" And that wasn't all that angered him. Once again King George and Parliament aggravated the situation in America. The Tea Act was passed, which forced colonists to buy tea *only* from a British tea company.

The Tea Act was too much.

The Sons of Liberty

Samuel Adams was from Boston. He was a representative in the Massachusetts legislature when the Stamp Act was passed in 1765. His cousin was John Adams, who later became America's second president. Samuel was much more hotheaded than his cousin. He was leader of a group called the Sons of Liberty. It urged colonists to rebel against Great Britain and unfair taxes. Other members included Patrick Henry, Paul Revere, and John Hancock.

These men met secretly to come up with ways to fight the king. The Sons of Liberty used propaganda to feed the anger of the colonists. Propaganda is information that tries to convince people of certain ideas. Adams and his friends used posters, newspaper cartoons, and pamphlets to show how unfair the king and his laws were.

Sam Adams had a knack for stirring up crowds.

Sometimes this led to violence. Sometimes British customs officers were captured, then tarred and feathered. Colonists poured hot tar on them and then covered them with feathers. And the homes of some British commissioners and military leaders were destroyed.

Not all the Sons of Liberty were in favor of these violent acts. But America's freedom from Great Britain and King George III was Sam Adams's only goal. He was one of the most popular and most important leaders of the American Revolution.

In Boston, the Sons of Liberty met daily to find a way to stop the Tea Act. In late November 1773, they saw their chance.

Three British ships docked in Boston Harbor carrying hundreds of chests of tea. Armed with guns, Sam Adams and the Sons of Liberty immediately lined the harbor. They did not let the British unload the tea from the ships.

Every day and every night, Boston citizens kept watch at the harbor, making sure the tea stayed right where it was.

The standoff lasted for more than two weeks. Then, on December 16, 1773, Adams and the Sons of Liberty decided it was time to do something daring. They would get rid of the tea once and for all!

That very night, some two hundred men and teenage boys disguised themselves as Native Americans. The crowd marched onto the docks at Boston Harbor. Because only a few British

soldiers were guarding the docks and ships, they put up no fight. They let the large, armed crowd board the three boats. In four hours, the protestors dumped over three hundred crates of tea—forty-six tons of tea leaves—into the bay! There was one heck of a tea party that night.

The colonists had broken the law by destroying British goods. Colonists were frequently hanged for such crimes. However, the next day the mood in Boston was upbeat. The rebels felt they'd sent an important message to the king: They weren't going to stand for iron-handed control of the colonies anymore. Everyone involved in the Tea Party kept quiet about his part in the event. The men refused to admit anything when questioned by British authorities.

This was a time long before e-mail, before telephones, even before telegrams. It took a month for news of the Tea Party to reach Great Britain. When King George was told about all the wasted tea floating in Boston Harbor, he was mad. Boiling mad.

CHAPTER 5
The First Continental Congress

After the Tea Party, King George III wanted revenge. The king was going to teach the colonists in Massachusetts a lesson.

How did he punish them?

In 1774, he had Parliament pass new laws. The colonists called them the Intolerable Acts.

Intolerable means something so horrible you cannot stand it. Now Boston Harbor was closed off. This was one of the major harbors in the northern colonies—lots of countries sent ships to Boston to sell their goods. Boston was the third largest city in the colonies (behind Philadelphia and New York), so lots of business and trade took place in the city. The king decided there would be no trading until the Massachusetts colony paid back the money lost from dumping all that tea. (The tea was worth somewhere between one to two million dollars in today's money.)

Massachusetts was then put under the strict control of General Thomas Gage and the British army.

General Thomas Gage

Now all public meetings, like the ones Sam Adams organized, were against the law. And now, American colonists had to let British soldiers live in their homes.

The colonists were shocked by the Intolerable Acts. Imagine being forced to let soldiers of the king you hated live with you. Even colonists in faraway South Carolina and Georgia were furious about what was happening in Massachusetts.

Something had to be done.

In September 1774, representatives from all the colonies (except Georgia) began holding meetings in Carpenters' Hall in Philadelphia, Pennsylvania. Philadelphia was the biggest city in the colonies, so it made sense for everyone to meet there.

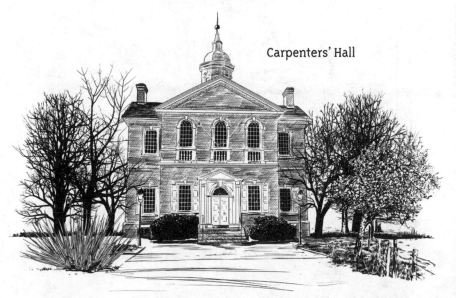

Carpenters' Hall

And Carpenters' Hall was located near the center of the city. The organizers decided it was better to meet somewhere other than Independence Hall—which was the state house—because too many members of the state house were supporters of the king. The colonists wanted to decide how, as one group, they should fight back against King George.

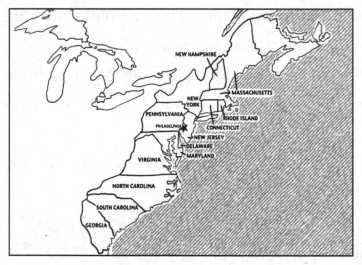

The meetings lasted two months and became known as the First Continental Congress. A congress is a meeting where people come to decide important questions of politics and law.

Of the fifty-six men who attended, some were already well known for their hatred of British rule: Sam and John Adams of Massachusetts, and Patrick Henry, Richard Lee, and George Washington, all from Virginia, were there.

Some representatives wanted to split from Great Britain completely—they wanted to govern themselves and create their own laws. Others hoped to make peace with Great Britain.

In the end, they reached a middle ground. A letter to King George III asked for the colonies to be represented in Parliament. Sam Adams thought asking this was a total waste of time.

Others, like Adams's cousin John, thought it was worth trying. The letter also asked for an end to all British taxes on the colonies, for Boston Harbor to be reopened, and for all British troops to leave the colonies immediately.

During the congress, the colonists also agreed to boycott all British goods for one year to try to show the king how serious they were about the demands in their letter.

The letter was delivered in November 1774. By January 1775, there had been no answer from the king or Parliament. Ben Franklin was in London at the time. He noted that the letter was presented in Parliament with a "heap" of others. But not much attention was paid to it.

Even months later, there was no official reply. King George

Ben Franklin

and Parliament simply ignored the letter. By saying nothing, the king was saying a lot!

This pushed the colonists further down the road to war. After the First Continental Congress, militias were formed in every colony.

A militia is a volunteer army that agrees to fight when needed. The delegates wanted to be sure that every colony was armed and prepared if the time came to fight the British.

The First Continental Congress ended in October 1774 with delegates agreeing to meet again the following year.

Patrick Henry (1736–1799)

Patrick Henry was at the First Continental Congress. The Virginia lawyer hated British rule over the colonies more than most—maybe even more than Sam Adams. Henry fought against the Stamp Act and the Townshend Acts by making speeches and writing articles in Virginia newspapers. His angry speeches made him a star of the First Continental Congress. He begged the other delegates to split from Great Britain completely.

A few months later, in March 1775, Patrick Henry delivered an amazing speech in his home colony. "I know not what course others may take," he said, "but as for me, give me liberty or give me death." Henry was willing to give up his life for freedom from Great Britain. His words quickly became a rallying cry for the increasing number of colonists against British rule.

When the Revolutionary War began, Henry organized militias in Virginia and forced the royal governor to leave the state. After the war, however, he opposed the Constitution, which laid out how the new United States government would work. That was because he believed in the right of states to make their own laws. He also said no to offers from both Presidents Washington and Adams to work for the new government. Henry died in 1799 at the age of sixty-three.

CHAPTER 6
The Shot Heard Round the World

After the First Continental Congress, a large, heavily armed militia formed in Massachusetts. The volunteer soldiers gathered up as many muskets, cannons, and as much gunpowder as possible. Of course, this was totally against the law. Remember, Boston was being punished for the Tea Party. Even town meetings had been

banned. But that didn't stop Sam Adams and others from planning for a revolt.

The question was: Where should they put all the weapons and gunpowder?

Concord, Massachusetts, seemed like the ideal place. It was a small quiet town about twenty miles northwest of Boston.

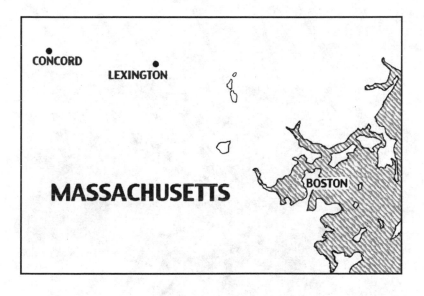

Unfortunately, British spies found out about the hidden weapons in Concord. General Thomas Gage decided to attack the colonists' stockpile.

This would crush their ability to fight against the king. But the colonists had their own spies. They learned when the redcoats—a nickname for the British soldiers because of their red uniforms—planned to raid Concord. It would be on the night of April 18, 1775.

British soldiers

Paul Revere

The colonial spies also learned which route the soldiers would take to get to Concord. It was Paul Revere who discovered that the British planned to sail up the Charles River to reach Concord. Revere and another man both mounted their horses and rode as fast as they could to Concord. They were able to warn the people guarding the weapons that the British troops were approaching.

In the early morning hours of April 19, 1775, a group of about seventy-five armed colonists faced off against seven hundred British soldiers near Lexington, which was about seven miles from Concord.

Someone—no one was sure who—shot his musket, and fighting began. Eight colonists were shot, and one British soldier was killed. The British army kept marching toward Concord.

What do you think the British army found there?

Nothing.

Because of Paul Revere's warning, all the weapons in Concord had been moved. The redcoats were so angry, they burned down many houses and shops.

Then they headed back to Boston. But on their way, the British soldiers ran into trouble. More than two thousand colonists—hiding behind houses, fences, and bushes—started shooting. The outnumbered British army quickly fled. Even in Lexington, where more British soldiers joined the fight, the colonists proved to be too strong. The British ran for their lives.

This was the first real battle in what soon turned into a war.

CHAPTER 7
The King Must Go

When word of the battle between the Massachusetts colonists and the redcoats spread to the other colonies, fear took over. Great Britain had the most powerful army in the world. How could the ragtag militias possibly defeat the Brits in an all-out war?

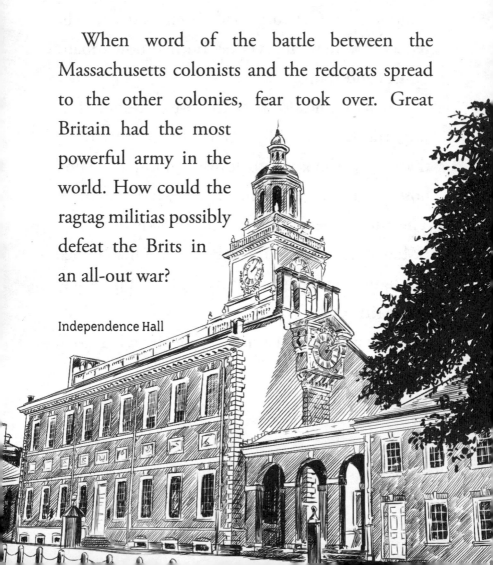

Independence Hall

Only a few weeks later, the Second Continental Congress met in Philadelphia. This time they met in Independence Hall. And this time, delegates from all thirteen colonies attended—fifty-six men in all.

Some were lawyers, some were businessmen, and some were farmers. Many of them were wealthy—some, like John Hancock from Massachusetts, were extremely wealthy. All were leaders in their colonies. As at the First Continental Congress the year before, some delegates still held out hope for a peaceful solution.

John Hancock

Where Were the Women?

Were there any women at either the First or Second Continental Congress?

No.

Back then, no woman was considered the equal of a man. Although colonial women joined protest groups against the king, and some even fought (in disguise) after the war broke out, they were not intended to have any of the rights that colonial men so desperately wanted—the right to vote, make laws, and control their own destinies. In the United States, women did not get the vote until 1920.

There were some new delegates to the Second Continental Congress. Benjamin Franklin, a well-known writer, printer, and inventor, was one. He urged the colonies to split from Great Britain. So did Thomas Jefferson, a farmer and scholar from Virginia.

Both of these men were gifted speakers. At the Second Continental Congress, they helped persuade others to their way of thinking and helped changed the course of America's history.

Thomas Jefferson

During the summer of 1775, the Second Continental Congress made many important decisions, including:

- creating a real army—not just militias—to fight against the British.
- voting George Washington from Virginia as the commander of the new army.

- printing their own money and refusing to use the British pound.

- organizing a navy to fight against Great Britain's powerful ships.
- sending Silas Deane from Connecticut to France to ask for help and money to fight the British.

In July 1775, the Second Continental Congress sent King George III another letter. The delegates were making one last try to avoid war. John Dickinson of Philadelphia wrote the letter.

He believed the colonies should stay connected to Great Britain. At the end, Dickinson wrote: "That your Majesty may enjoy a long and prosperous reign, and that your descendants may govern your Dominions with honour to themselves and happiness to their subjects, is our sincere prayer." Dickinson's letter was saying that the colonists hoped King George would rule over America for a long time and bring happiness to everyone.

What did Sam Adams, Ben Franklin, Patrick Henry, and Thomas Jefferson think of Dickinson's letter to King George III?

They despised the idea.

John Dickinson

But the letter was sent anyway

How did King George react? He refused to read the letter. He wouldn't even look at it.

The king's silence convinced even delegates who had hoped for peace that staying connected to Great Britain was no longer possible.

Thomas Paine's *Common Sense*

Thomas Paine was a British man who came to America in 1774 with the help of Benjamin Franklin. Paine was inspired by what the colonists were doing to combat the British army. In January 1776, he published a forty-eight-page pamphlet called *Common Sense*. Paine argued—in plain language— why America should split from Great Britain. *Common Sense* became the best-selling pamphlet in America. Half a million copies were bought. That meant at least one out of every four colonists read it. Paine's words were read out loud in pubs and meeting halls throughout the colonies. General George Washington had *Common Sense* read to his soldiers. Thomas Paine could have made a fortune from his pamphlet. But he accepted no money from its sales. He gave nearly all profits to the American army for uniforms and weapons.

CHAPTER 8
Declaring Freedom

What needed to be done next was clear: The American colonies had to tell the king that they demanded to be their own country—apart from Great Britain.

The notice they sent the king would have to make it completely clear that the colonies had no choice but to go to war. They did not expect the king to be persuaded by anything they said. But they did want other countries to understand that the colonies had been forced to rebel against the king of Great Britain. But who was best suited to write something so important and dangerous?

The members of the Second Continental Congress turned to five men—Ben Franklin of Pennsylvania, John Adams of Massachusetts, Robert Livingston of New York, Roger Sherman of Connecticut, and Thomas Jefferson of Virginia.

The group thought Jefferson should write it by himself instead of trying to do it together. Jefferson wasn't so sure about that. He and Adams were close friends. Why didn't Adams try writing it? But John Adams wouldn't do it because, as he told Jefferson, "You can write ten times better than I can."

So the job fell to Thomas Jefferson. For two weeks he worked on the first draft of the Declaration of Independence. He was renting a second-floor room in the home of a Philadelphia bricklayer. The house was on the outskirts of town—Jefferson wanted to be away from the noise of the city. He used a quill pen that he had to keep dipping in a bottle of ink. And he wrote on large, oversize sheets of paper. He wrote early each morning, stopping when his room became too hot.

Pen, Ink, and Parchment

Today pens are manufactured so cheaply that losing one or having it run out of ink is no big deal. However, in the 1700s, writers made their own pens. They used a quill, one of the large feathers from the wing or tail of a bird. Quills from geese, crows, or swans were commonly used. Thomas Jefferson owned special geese so he'd never run out of supplies. The tip of the quill was sharpened with a knife to make a pen point. And then the quill was dipped in ink. Ink was made from all kinds of things, like berry juice or even soot from the fireplace. The signers of the declaration used iron-gall ink from melted metal and plants. Important documents weren't written on paper but on parchment, which was made from dried animal skin. The Declaration of Independence on display at the Library of Congress is on parchment.

Rich colonists who didn't want to make writing supplies by hand could buy them from a shopkeeper. Traders often sold fancy European quills, ink, and parchment at the local seaports.

Later in the day, Jefferson spent time with other delegates from across the colonies.

Even though he was kind of a quiet man, Jefferson talked a lot about the declaration. With his friends Franklin and Adams he frequently discussed exactly what needed to be included.

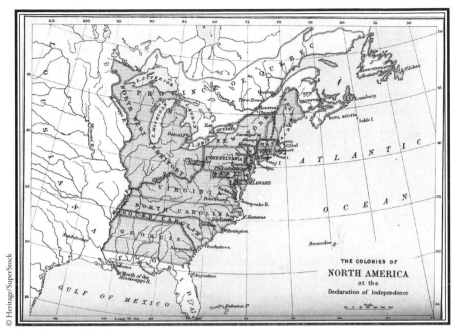

© Heritage/SuperStock

The colonies of North America at the time of the declaration

© Universal Images Group/SuperStock

An illustration of the Stamp Act riots of 1765

© Don Troiani/Corbis

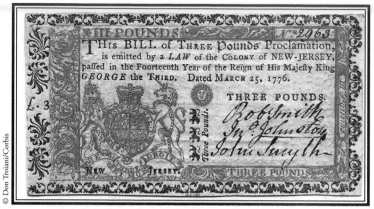

A New Jersey three-pound note

© The Art Archive/SuperStock

Portrait of King George III of England

A depiction of the Boston Massacre on March 5, 1770

Illustration of Samuel Adams

© SuperStock

An artist's rendering of the Boston Tea Party on December 16, 1773

© James P. Blair/Exactostock-1598/SuperStock

Paul Revere's house in Boston's North End neighborhood

Paul Revere warns of British troops in this painting
by artist Charles C. J. Hoffbauer

© SuperStock

© Bridgman Art Library/SuperStock

Portrait of George Washington as American general

A depiction of the Battle of Lexington on April 19, 1775

Independence Hall in Philadelphia, Pennsylvania

© Wynnter/Thinkstock

Portrait of Thomas Jefferson, author of the Declaration of Independence

Portrait of Robert R. Livingston, one of five congressional
members appointed to write the declaration

Portrait of Benjamin Franklin

© ACME Imagery/SuperStock

Portrait of John Adams

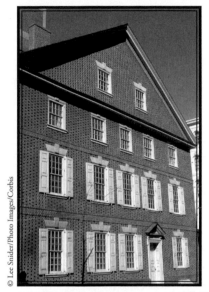

© Lee Snider/Photo Images/Corbis

A reconstruction of the Graff House in Philadelphia,
where Jefferson wrote the Declaration of Independence

© Francis G. Mayer/Corbis

An illustration of the signing of the Declaration of Independence
by artist John Trumbull

© Universal Images Group/SuperStock

THE REBELS OF '76.
THE GREAT

July 4 1776

OR, THE FIRST ANNOUNCEMENT OF
DECLARATION.

The Second Continental Congress announces the signing of the declaration to residents of Philadelphia in this nineteenth-century print.

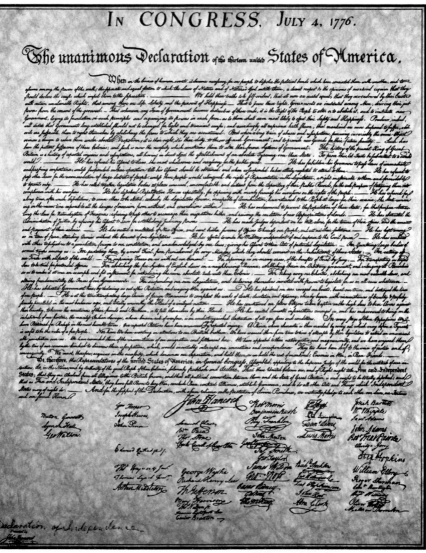

A replica of the Declaration of Independence

© SuperStock

A painting of George Washington leading his troops in 1778

© Mark Alberhasky/SuperStock

Fireworks traditionally celebrate the Fourth of July

Sometimes, when he returned in the evening to his room, Jefferson would crumple up what he had written before and start over. The declaration would start a war. Jefferson understood that fellow colonists would die because of his words.

Jefferson was a scholar, a man of learning. He had read many, many books and written many papers on various subjects. He was a student of the

Enlightenment. It was a period of time between the mid-1600s and late 1700s when men turned to the power and truth of science over what they saw as the superstition of religion. He had read many of the great thinkers of the day such as John Locke of Great Britain. Locke put forth a daring idea: that human beings are born with certain rights, and these rights cannot be given or taken away by kings. Thomas Paine's *Common Sense* also made a big impact on Jefferson.

In writing the Declaration of Independence, Jefferson tried to combine ideas of new thinkers with the political goals of the American colonies. The Declaration of Independence had to do two important things: 1) explain why the colonies needed to break away from Great Britain and King George, and 2) describe what the new country stood for.

Thomas Jefferson wrote the Declaration of Independence in four parts.

The first part was an introduction explaining that the declaration would show why the colonies needed to be free.

In the second part, Jefferson laid out the ideas on which the new country would be built. After living without representation in Parliament, the new country would be governed only by "the consent of the governed." That meant citizens would have a say in what the new government did. And every man would have the right to

"Life, Liberty and the pursuit of Happiness." This is the most famous part of the Declaration of Independence. (Again, remember, it is talking about "men"—women were not going to be full citizens allowed to vote.)

The third part was the longest. In it Jefferson lists all the unfair things Parliament and the king did to the colonies—imposing taxes, stopping trade, closing down colonial governments, and forcing colonists to let British soldiers live in their homes. The king had heard all this before, but Jefferson wanted the whole world to see how badly Great Britain had treated the colonies.

In the final part, Jefferson introduces the name of the new country—the United States of America. He also clearly states that Great Britain will have no control over the United States. None at all.

Jefferson was pleased enough with what he had written to show it to Ben Franklin and

John Adams. Both suggested a few very minor changes, which Jefferson made. The Declaration of Independence was ready to be presented to the Second Continental Congress.

Richard Lee's Declaration

Richard Lee was a wealthy Virginian and a strong opponent of King George III. Lee wrote articles and fought against the Stamp Act and the Intolerable Acts. He also helped organize groups in different colonies that worked together to fight against the British.

Lee's hatred for the British was clearly on display during the Second Continental Congress. On June 7, 1776, Lee proposed the following:

Resolved: that these United Colonies are, and of right ought to be, free and independent States, that they are absolved from all allegiance to the British Crown, and that all political connection between them and the state of Great Britain is, and ought to be totally dissolved.

Many members of the Second Continental Congress agreed with Lee, but not enough colonies were willing to support Lee's proposal to pass it. However, Thomas Jefferson was so impressed with Lee's powerful proposal that he used the exact wording in the Declaration of Independence to announce that the United States of America would be completely free from Great Britain.

CHAPTER 9
The United States of America Is Born

Now that the declaration was written, the question was: How would the delegates react?

On June 28, 1776, Thomas Jefferson delivered the Declaration of Independence to the Second Continental Congress. Jefferson did not like to speak in public because he had a lisp and was very self-conscious about it. So he did not read the

declaration—he gave the written parchment to the president of the congress, John Hancock. Delegates took turns gathering around the parchment to read the words Jefferson had written.

It created a *huge* buzz. *Everyone* had an opinion.

But before any official debate on the declaration, the Congress had to vote again on Richard Lee's proposal of independence. On July 2, 1776, it passed! The colonists had officially decided to break free of Great Britain and King George III.

Who Thought Up the Country's Name?

Unfortunately, it is not clear exactly who first called the new country the United States of America. Jefferson used it as the title of one of his first versions of the declaration. But in the final draft he changed it slightly to the "thirteen United States of America." Other people definitely used the name before the declaration was written. For example, three months earlier, in March of 1776, a farmer in Virginia had written letters to a local newspaper referring to the United States of America. And a couple of months before that, one of Washington's officers used the same name in a letter about hoping to travel to Spain to get that country's help for the war to create the United States of America.

John Adams was so excited about the vote on Lee's declaration that he quickly wrote a letter to his wife, Abigail. He said that July 2 would be celebrated across the colonies as the birth of the new nation for years to come. Adams was only two days off.

Then the debate started on the declaration. And very quickly, Thomas Jefferson grew annoyed. He sat in the steamy assembly room where the Second Continental Congress was meeting, and

listened to delegates pick apart his words. This is hard for all writers. The delegates debated with passion and sometimes even anger. To Jefferson, it was like having fifty-five editors making changes to something that *they* asked *him* to write.

Some changes were minor and didn't bother Jefferson at all. But other changes made Jefferson furious. He had originally included language condemning slavery. Most of the delegates from the South, including Jefferson, owned slaves. But he felt strongly that this new country—based on freedom—could not allow slavery to continue. Jefferson argued to keep the antislavery language in the declaration. But too many Southern delegates said that, if so, they would not sign the declaration. John Adams and Ben Franklin, who agreed with Jefferson about slavery, convinced him that it was better to compromise than to have no declaration and no new country. Jefferson fumed, but he agreed. So the language ending slavery was cut.

The fierce debate over the Declaration of Independence lasted three days. It might have lasted longer if it weren't for the horseflies that pestered the delegates throughout their meetings. (There was a stable nearby, and swarms of the flies came through the open windows.) There were nearly one hundred changes, making the declaration 25 percent shorter than Jefferson's original. Jefferson returned to his room and wrote out a final version. He delivered it to the Second Continental Congress on the morning of July 4, 1776. There was no more debate. No more arguments. At this point, only two men signed the document—John Hancock, the president of the Continental Congress, and Charles Thompson, the congressional secretary.

The United States of America was born.

Hancock sent the document to a local printer to have about two hundred copies made. By July 5, they were being delivered to all the colonies.

One copy went to George Washington in New York, where he was stationed with his troops. (Ever since the fighting in Lexington and Concord in

the spring of 1775, there had been small battles going on between the Continental Army and the redcoats, especially in the Northeast.)

On July 8, the Declaration of Independence was read aloud to a crowd outside Independence Hall. A bell rang repeatedly, and everyone cheered wildly.

The following day, General Washington had the declaration read to his troops and New York colonists. The large crowd was so excited that they pulled down a fifteen-foot-tall statue of King George III on a horse.

Legend has it that the statue was melted down to make more than forty thousand bullets for the American army.

In mid-July, the congress ordered a new, more clearly written copy of the declaration. This was what all fifty-six delegates to the Second Continental Congress signed. A Pennsylvania man named Timothy Matlock copied the declaration in clean handwriting on large parchment paper (about two feet by two and a half feet).

On August 2, 1776, this official version of the Declaration of Independence was presented to John Hancock, the president of the Congress. He was the first to sign. Fifty delegates joined Hancock that day in signing the document. (Five other delegates signed it at a later date.)

The Revolutionary War began. And the brand-new United States of America had to win it. Losing was *not* possible.

John Hancock's Signature

For the past two hundred years, the phrase "put your John Hancock here" means writing one's signature. That's because Hancock's name on the Declaration of Independence can't be missed—it's the largest and centered directly under the text. According to legend, Hancock wanted his name to be big enough so the king could see it without putting on his glasses. But many historians say that is only a story. They suggest that the real reason Hancock's signature is so big is that he signed it first—he didn't think about the fact that fifty-five other signatures had to fit in the empty space below the text.

CHAPTER 10
What Happened to the Signers?

All the men who wrote their names on the Declaration of Independence knew they were putting their lives on the line. The simple act of writing their signatures meant they might be executed. After the witty Benjamin Franklin signed his name, he is reported to have said, "We must all hang together, or assuredly we shall all hang separately." By this he meant that the signers all had to stick together because, if the redcoats caught them, they would each be hung as a traitor.

Some of these men did indeed pay with their lives. Five of the signers were captured and held prisoner by the British during the war. A dozen or more had their houses attacked and burned. Others had their businesses destroyed.

The home of Francis Lewis of New York was raided by the British while he was still at the Second Continental Congress in Philadelphia. His wife was taken prisoner and held for several months. Later she was freed in exchange for the release of British soldiers held by American forces.

The war was not a short one. General Washington and his troops defeated the British army at Yorktown in October 1781. After that, the war was essentially over. But it would take two more years before a peace treaty was signed. With victory for the United States of America, the real work as outlined in the Declaration of Independence began. Making one nation out of thirteen colonies with different needs and interests was not an easy job. For that, another even more important document had to be written—the United States Constitution in 1787.

Many of the men who signed the declaration were eager to serve in the new government. Sam Adams became governor of Massachusetts for more than three years.

John Hancock also was elected governor of Massachusetts many times between 1780 and 1793, the year he died. Richard Henry Lee was appointed one of the first senators from Virginia after the Constitution was passed. Benjamin Franklin, who played an important role in shaping the Constitution, was appointed the first United States postmaster general.

Others among the signers rose to even higher offices.

John Adams served as vice president under the very first president, George Washington. Then in 1796, Adams was elected the second president of the United States. He served for four years—he and his wife, Abigail, moved into the brand-new White House in Washington, DC, in 1800.

Thomas Jefferson became Secretary of State under President Washington. He lost the presidential election of 1796 to John Adams, but he got enough votes to become vice president.

The White House

They did not agree on how the government should be run. Jefferson became the third president of the United States in 1801. He served two terms. Ironically, both Jefferson and John Adams died on the same day—July 4, 1826, exactly fifty years after the Declaration of Independence was signed by John Hancock.

Famous or not, each of the signers are heroes who put their lives on the line and played a part in founding our country.

The Signers

Connecticut
Roger Sherman
Samuel Huntington
William Williams
Oliver Wolcott

Delaware
George Read
Thomas McKean
Caesar Rodney

Georgia
Button Gwinnett
Lyman Hall
George Walton

Maryland
Charles Carroll
Samuel Chase
William Paca
Thomas Stone

Massachusetts
John Adams
Samuel Adams
Elbridge Gerry
John Hancock
Robert Treat Paine

New Hampshire
Josiah Bartlett
Matthew Thornton
William Whipple

New Jersey
Abraham Clark
John Hart
Francis Hopkinson
Richard Stockton
John Witherspoon

New York

William Floyd

Francis Lewis

Philip Livingston

Lewis Morris

North Carolina

Joseph Hewes

William Hooper

John Penn

Pennsylvania

George Clymer

Benjamin Franklin

(the *oldest* signer

at seventy)

Robert Morris

John Morton

George Ross

Benjamin Rush

James Smith

George Taylor

James Wilson

Rhode Island

William Ellery

Stephen Hopkins

South Carolina

Thomas Heyward, Jr.

Thomas Lynch, Jr.

Arthur Middleton

Edward Rutledge

(the *youngest* signer

at twenty-six)

Virginia

Carter Braxton

Benjamin Harrison

Thomas Jefferson

Francis Lightfoot Lee

Richard Henry Lee

Thomas Nelson, Jr.

George Wythe

CHAPTER 11
The Declaration Today

The Declaration of Independence is one of the most important political documents ever written in all of human history. It has inspired people around the world to demand their freedom in the 240 years since it was written.

After it was signed in 1776, the original Declaration of Independence was moved many, many times to different locations. Since 1952 it has been kept at the National Archives building in Washington, DC, where tourists may see it.

The document is very faded and has suffered a lot of damage over the years. Even so, you can still read some of the names of the people who signed the declaration, especially John Hancock's large signature.

Independence Hall in Philadelphia, where the declaration was signed, is a National Park Service site that you can visit. You can sit in the assembly room and imagine what it was like when the founders of our country argued over what the new United States would be like.

Unfortunately, the house where Thomas Jefferson rented a room and wrote the declaration was torn down in 1883. However, based on photos taken in the late 1800s, the National Park Service was able to re-create the building and room in 1975.

It is open to visitors. A key to Jefferson's desk is one of the few original items there. Who knows—maybe Jefferson used the key to lock up his drafts of the original declaration. If so, it's one of the most important keys in US history!

Timeline of the Declaration of Independence

1754	The French and Indian War begins
1760	King George III ascends to the throne on October 25
1761	Great Britain imposes the Writs of Assistance on the colonies
1764	Great Britain's Sugar Act taxes the colonists' use of sugar, molasses, wine, lumber, and iron
1765	The Stamp Act taxes all paper documents (even playing cards) in the colonies
1767	The Townshend Acts impose a tax on paint, glass, oil, lead, and tea. They cause so many protests that they are later repealed—except for the tax on tea
1770	Unarmed colonists are killed by British soldiers in the Boston Massacre
1773	Great Britain passes the Tea Act, forcing colonists to buy tea from a British company. Colonists revolt and stage the Boston Tea Party
1774	Parliament passes the Intolerable Acts. The colonies protest fiercely. The First Continental Congress meets in Philadelphia. All the colonies except Georgia send delegates
1775	The "shot heard round the world" is fired near Lexington, Massachusetts. The Revolutionary War begins. The Second Continental Congress meets in Philadelphia, with all colonies represented. A Continental Army is formed with George Washington as its commander in chief
1776	The Congress votes to break free of Great Britain. Thomas Jefferson writes the Declaration of Independence, which is adopted on July 4
1778	France agrees to send troops and money to the United States of America to help defeat the British and King George III
1783	The Revolutionary War officially ends—the United States of America is an independent country

Timeline of the World

1751	—	The publication of the *Encyclopédie* begins in France and highly influences Enlightenment thinkers
1753	—	Ben Franklin invents the lightning rod in America to protect against electrical charge of lightning bolts
1756	—	Wolfgang Amadeus Mozart is born in Salzburg, Austria
1760	—	The Industrial Revolution begins in Great Britain
1762	—	Catherine the Great becomes the empress of Russia
1765	—	James Watt invents the steam engine
1769	—	France's future leader Napoleon Bonaparte is born
	—	Captain James Cook claims New Zealand for Great Britain
1774	—	Louis XVI ascends to the throne in France
1776	—	Adam Smith publishes the first book of his economic theory, *The Wealth of Nations*
1779	—	The first iron bridge is built in Shropshire, Great Britain
1783	—	King George III declares the American colonies free and independent
1787	—	The US Constitution is written and voted on in Philadelphia, Pennsylvania

Bibliography

*Books for young readers

*Fradin, Dennis. *The Declaration of Independence.* Chicago: Children's Press, 1988.

*Fradin, Dennis. *The Signers: The 56 Stories Behind the Declaration of Independence.* New York: Walker & Company, 2002.

Freedman, Russell. *Give Me Liberty!: The Story of the Declaration of Independence.* New York: Holiday House, 2000.

*Graves, Kerry A. *The Declaration of Independence: The Story Behind America's Founding Document.* Philadelphia: Chelsea Clubhouse, 2004.

Malone, Dumas, *The Story of the Declaration of Independence.* New York: Oxford, 1954.

*Micklos, John. *From Thirteen Colonies to One Nation.* Berkley Heights, NJ: Enslow, 2008.

Miller, Brandon Marie. *Declaring Independence: Life During the American Revolution.* Minneapolis: Lerner, 2005.

*Oberle, Lora. *The Declaration of Independence.* Mankato, MN: Capstone Press, 2002.

*Richards, Norman. *The Story of the Declaration of Independence.* Chicago: Children's Press, 1968.

Taylor, Dale. *The Writer's Guide to Everyday Life in Colonial America, From 1607-1783.* Cincinnati: Writer's Digest Books, 1997.